SALTLESS
LOW SALT COOKING

COMFORT
FOOD

COOKBOOK: LOW SALT RECIPES
LOW SODIUM HOME COOKING

HARPER FULLERTON
UNITED KINGDOM

Copyright

CONTENTS

A L L
I N   T H E   F A M I L Y

'Saltless is for people who love good food and love cooking. And for those who realize that good food and good heath are compatible. Salt is hard to give up because it's a vehicle for flavor. Low salt diets often fail because just taking salt out of dishes makes the food tasteless. Boring food puts your taste buds to sleep. Eating should be a pleasure not taken as a spoonful of medicine. That's why Saltless is all about recipes that are not only low in salt, but really delicious in flavor.

Recent research shows, that anxiety from counting salt grams, increases the body's craving for salty foods. In fact, stress actually makes your body retain salt. Dr. Gregory Harshfield of Georgia Health Sciences University says, "Every time a person is stressed, they hold onto as much salt as you get when you eat a small order of French fries. And this can occur many times over the course of a day". In Saltless you'll find specific details on sodium content which relieves you of the anxiety of counting salt. We have made the counting salt grams our job so you can get on with the love of preparing delicious quick and easy low salt meals.

The question is can "lack" of salt coexist with delicious flavors? Yes it can. By adapting and testing new versions of recipes you can now change the salt habit of a lifetime. We know that eating tasty, gutsy food without salt, is truly one of life's great pleasures.

WHY SALT IS THE BAD BOY OF FOOD

Let's say your idea of a perfect weekend is this. Drinking coffee, reading a newspaper and starting your Saturday with a full English or American breakfast. The 100gms of crispy bacon, more if you sneaked a few rashers while you were grilling it - contains 1021mg/sodium. The two fried or scrambled farm eggs 148mg/sodium, butter 826mg/sodium, two slices of toast 500mg/sodium, two small grilled tomatoes 130 mg/sodium and a serving of baked beans 436 mg/sodium. The grand total for Sunday breakfast is 3061 mg/sodium. A diet high in salt increases the risk of heart disease, strokes, high blood pressure and many other medical conditions.

Making food choices which are low in salt, can help you reduce symptoms, improve health and maintain a healthy active lifestyle with less health problems.

Maintaining a sodium intake below 2000mg is a matter of making the right food choices. So the aim of a low sodium diet is to move the regulation system towards the lowest point of its range without pushing it to its limit and causing the actual sodium levels in the body to fail. If the low salt diet is taken to extremes, it can have an adverse reaction. Extremely low levels would need to be monitored by a doctor. It's not just about salt you can see. There is hidden salt in many products, even the daily loaf of bread and tomato sauce. Read the food labels on cans and packets. The amount of salt is listed as sodium. Read the labels and compare sodium content. The difference can be huge. Buy the lowest sodium content on every item.

Avoid salty foods such as processed meats and fish, pickles, relish, sauces especially soy sauce, salted nuts, chips and processed snack foods. Pretzels 1680mg/sodium per 100 grams, potato chips up to 1000mg / sodium a portion. Foods that come in a tin or packet or ready cooked, like spaghetti sauce in a jar or dried soup in a packet, are usually high in salt. Beef and chicken stock cubes have 24,000mg of sodium per 100 grams. Dried beef 4,300mg/sodium. Look for products that have the lowest sodium content, based on the amount you eat. You will see the nutritional box on the packet or tin. Many high sodium products such as tomato sauce show low sodium values because the sodium is based on small sodium portions.

Many manufacturers are producing low salt products such as salt reduced baked beans, sodium reduced tuna fish and low salt feta cheese. Read the labels carefully before you buy. Avoid cooking with salt or adding salt to the cooking.

TEN
LOW SALT
COOKING
TIPS

Cooking is a creative process and ingredients are interchangeable. If you don't have a specific ingredient, use the glossary in this book to find a substitute. When you do this, you'll create a signature dish of your own.

You can use the recipes in this book to whip up a meal with a minimum of fuss. By using fresh foods, preferably organic, you can cook dishes that taste great without salt. So, as much as possible, eat what is in season. Grow your own herbs.Use the freshest spices. Shop in local markets for the seasonal produce.

1. Use herbs and spices instead of salt.
2. Marinades and sauces don't have to include salt, soy sauce, barbecue sauce, tamari or fish sauce. Leave them out.
3. Let stocks, soups and stews cook slowly or on simmer to enhance flavor.
4. Cook stews and casseroles the day before and reheat the next day to increase flavor intensity.
5. Use stocks or wine instead of water in casseroles, soups and braised dishes.
6. Cook grains like rice and beans in stock; add herbs, garlic, and onions for a rich flavor.
7. Defat pan juices which are left after cooking. Then simply add wine or water to deglaze the frying pan on low heat. Use these juices as a flavorful sauce.
8. Make sauces from reduced meat or vegetable stocks. Add fresh herbs, season with pepper and thicken with corn flour.
9. Cook with condiments like homemade no salt added chutneys and preserves to give a glaze to roasted meats, grilled or barbecued food.
10. Don't throw out your favorite old recipes. Use the sections in this book to substitute other ingredients for salt and enjoy your familiar flavors.

THE HEALTHY PANTRY

30 LOW SALT ITEMS TO STOCK YOUR FRIDGE, FREEZER OR PANTRY

1. Homemade no salt chicken stock, meat and vegetable stock
2. Dairy: yogurt, butter, eggs
3. No salt homemade mozzarella, ricotta cheese, mascarpone, crème fraiche
4. Fresh herbs. (Grow in containers or in the garden)
5. Rice, pasta of all shapes
6. Beans, lentils and dried legumes, grains
7. Oil for cooking: olive oil
8. Oil for flavor: cold-pressed walnut, extra virgin olive oil, hazelnut, sesame
9. Tomato paste, tomato puree, tinned tomatoes
10. Vinegars: red, white, balsamic, herb infused

11. Onions, shallots, green onions, garlic, ginger

12. Lemons, limes, oranges

13. Long life vegetables: pumpkin, potatoes

14. Whole grain bread

15. Organic unbleached white flour

16. Low sodium baking powder

17. Nuts: hazelnuts, almonds.

18. Rolled oats

19. Black, white, green and dried peppercorns

20. Mushrooms: Porcini, button, brown, Portobello

21. Homemade no salt tomato sauce, barbecue sauce, chutneys

22. Wines: red and white

23. Salt free corn chips and crackers

24. Grains, wheat, couscous

25. Frozen berries: strawberries, blueberries, raspberries, and blackberries

26. Frozen organic chicken, organic steak, wild caught salmon fillets, wild caught white fish

27. Seasonal vegetables to keep in the fridge: carrots, lettuces, rocket leaves, baby spinach, celery and beetroot

28. In the freezer: no salt pizza bases

29. Exotic ingredients: quince paste, vanilla bean

30. Vegetables: peas, soya beans, green beans

SUBSTITUTE FOODS

SUBSTITUTE HIGH SALT FOODS FOR LOW SALT FOODS

Salt
Replace with: kelp has natural iodine which gives a natural saltiness to food without the high sodium of table salt so it makes a good substitute for a low salt diet. Available in flakes, granules, dried and powder.

Cornstarch
Replace with arrowroot from the arrowroot plant.

Phosphate baking powder
Phosphate baking powder has a high sodium content Replace with low salt tartrate baking powder.

Double acting baking powder

Replace with low salt aluminum-free baking powder.

Baking soda

Replace with low-sodium aluminum-free baking powder (use two parts baking powder in place of one part soda for baking muffins, cookies, cakes and breads).

White sugar

Replace with raw sugar or a dark sugar; or raw honey, 1/2 cup of honey = 1 cup of white sugar (reduce the amount of liquid in the recipe by 1/4 of a cup and add an extra 3 tbsp of flour). Use pure maple syrup, fruit juices, purees, applesauce, mashed bananas, apple juice concentrate in recipes. 1 cup of white sugar = 1/2 cup apple juice concentrate. 1 cup of raw sugar = 1 cup of palm sugar.

Soft drinks

Replace with hot iced fruit teas, herbal teas, fruit juice, vegetable juice, mineral water (non-carbonated, low/sodium).

Chicken stock cubes

Replace with one cup of no-salt chicken broth made from chicken bones simmered one hour in water with vegetables and strained. You can freeze this in small, usable portions. Or use commercially prepared no-salt stock.

Beef bouillon cubes

Replace with home-made beef stock. Take beef marrow bones and roast them in the oven 200 degrees C for 30 minutes. Add water to the pan to take up the released juices. Place juice from pan and bones into a soup pot. Add vegetables such as carrots and onions to flavor the stock. Cover bones with 1 liter of water and simmer bones and vegetables, lid off, for one hour on low heat. Cool and strain.

Garlic powder

Replace with 1 clove of garlic crushed. Make a garlic paste. Roast the whole head of garlic in the oven until it softens to a paste. Use the paste in soups, vegetables, sandwiches and soups instead of garlic powder. Keep in the fridge.

Steak seasonings, barbecue seasonings and other commercial shaker seasonings

Replace with homemade seasonings.

Peanut butter

Replace with a no-salt brand.

Canned and packet soups

Replace with salt-free home-made meat, chicken, vegetable, fish broths and soups made from bones, herbs and vegetables.

Canned vegetables

Replace with raw, fresh or no-salt frozen/canned vegetables.

Dried fruits

Commercial dried fruits such as prunes, raisins, apricots and cranberries contain preservative. Replace with fruits which are dried without preservative.

White flour

Replace with: organic unbleached white flour, wholemeal, corn, rye, oat flour, buckwheat, rice flour. Avoid all white processed food products such as commercial cakes and biscuits.

Black tea and iced tea

Replace with green tea such as jasmine tea, fruit tea, spice and herb teas sweetened with a little honey.

Caffeinated coffee

Replace with quality brand of water processed decaffeinated coffee. If you have been drinking a lot of tea and coffee, substitute other beverages slowly to avoid a caffeine headache! Start with lemon juice in water each morning and then replace one cup of coffee or tea for a herbal tea.

Cereal

Most commercial cereals have excessive amounts of salt and sugar. Replace with oats and home-made granola and muesli.

Jam and jellies

Commercial jams are loaded with sugar. Replace with home-made fruit spread. Cut up the fruit of your choice, apples, peaches, nectarines, mangoes or berries. Puree them in a food processor, adding a little honey if they are tart. You can add lemon or lime juice and spices such as cardamom or cinnamon. Place the pureed fruit in a greased, flat baking dish and bake in a very low oven 150 degree C until thick, for 2-4 hours. Keep in a jar in the fridge. Quick fruit puree - follow the recipe above but cook over low heat in a saucepan with a little honey or maple syrup to make a honey fruit or maple fruit jam. Prune jam - cook dried prunes in a little water and orange juice and a cinnamon stick. Remove cinnamon stick. Cool and puree to make prune jam.

Sweetened yogurt

Replace with plain yogurt (preferably organic or home-made) sweeten with honey and a teaspoon of vanilla, apple sauce with cinnamon, maple syrup, apricot nectar, peach nectar, stewed dried apricots, prunes, peaches, pineapple, apple fruit concentrate, muesli and granola, almonds and honey.

Canned beans and spaghetti

Replace with cooked beans without salt.

Cheeses, hard cheeses, parmesan, and cheese

spreads

Replace with no-salt cottage cheese, no-salt ricotta or soft tofu. Make your own no-salt cheese. Take 2 cups of fresh plain unsweetened acidophilus yogurt and chop your favorite herbs, chives, parsley, basil and mix until smooth then wrap the yogurt in a clean damp cotton muslin cloth. Suspend the "yogurt" above a bowl overnight and the juices will drain from the yogurt leaving a soft cheese in the morning. Chill and serve with crackers or bread, pita wraps or salads.

Anchovies, salted herrings

Replace with fresh white fish, tinned low salt tuna, fresh salmon.

Meats, smoked, pickled, corned beef, gravy, ham, salami, bologna, meat pastes and pate

Replace with fresh turkey, chicken, lamb, beef, pork.

Nuts, salted, roasted

Replace with unsalted popcorn, fresh raw nuts, pine nuts, pumpkin seeds, sunflower seeds.

Salted potato crisps, pretzels

Replace with home-made crisps using very thinly sliced potatoes or sweet potato. Place on an oven tray and drizzle with olive oil. Sprinkle with black pepper. Bake in a 200 degree C oven until golden brown and crisp.

THE SALTLESS HOME DAIRY

Mozzarella Cheese

One slice of bought whole milk mozzarella, can contain 178mg of sodium. One slice of saltless home made mozzarella, contains 5mg. Here is a recipe for homemade no salt mozzarella. You can make this recipe in 30 minutes. Less than the time it takes to go to the supermarket.

Makes: about 500g

Ingredients

4.5 liters of whole milk

1 1/2 tsp citric acid

1/4 tablet rennet

mineral water

* Do not use junket rennet for making mozzarella, as it is not strong enough.

Method

Mix citric acid in 1 cup cold water.

Pour milk into a heavy bottomed saucepan. Stir in citric acid mixture.

Heat the milk to 32 degrees C, stirring constantly. Remove from heat. Dissolve rennet tablet in 1/4 cup cool water. Add this slowly to the milk using an up and down motion with a slotted metal spoon. Cover with a lid. Let stand for 5 minutes. Remove lid and check the curd. It should resemble custard when pressed lightly with your finger.

Take a metal knife or spatula. Slice across the surface of the curd cutting the curd into 3cm squares. Return the saucepan to the heat and heat the curd to 40 degrees C, while slowly stirring the curd with your spoon. Remove from heat and stir for 2-5 minutes. The more you stir the firmer the mozzarella will be. Pour into a sieve or colander. The curds will drain off from the whey (the liquid). Pour curds into a microwavable bowl. Tip bowl to drain off whey. Microwave on high for 1 minute. Drain off the whey again. Microwave again for 30 seconds. Remove from bowl and place curds on a workbench. Knead, as you would bread dough, turning the cheese and folding the cheese over. Keep kneading until the cheese turns glossy. If cheese doesn't hold together, microwave for another 30 seconds on high.

Cheese is ready when it is so elastic that you can

stretch it into a long strand.

Form the cheese into a loaf shape or a ball. You can plait the cheese also. Then fill a bowl with cool water and submerge the cheese for 15 minutes. This will help the cheese keep its shape and maintain a silky texture.

Cheese keeps in the fridge in a covered container for up to 2 weeks. You can also wrap the cheese tightly in cling film and freeze it.

Hot Water Bath Directions

If you don't have a microwave you can create mozzarella by using the following method. Follow cheese-making steps in the recipe up to the microwave instructions. Instead of using the microwave, heat water in a heavy saucepan to 82 degrees C. Spoon the curds into a colander or sieve, folding the curds over gently as you drain off the whey. Dip the colander into the hot water several times. Take a spoon and fold the curds until they become elastic and pliable. Remove the curds, stretch and pull. If it does not stretch easily, return to the hot water bath in the colander and repeat the process. Then knead cheese until it is pliable. Submerge in water for 15 minutes. Drain.

Ricotta Cheese

Homemade ricotta cheese is as cheap to make as the cost of a liter of milk. Homemade ricotta makes a great base for ravioli fillings and lasagna. You can serve with freshly sliced fruit: peaches, nectarines and berries. Or with stewed stone fruit: apricots, plums or fresh figs served with a drizzle of honey.

Makes: 2 cups
Cooking time: 30 minutes

Ingredients

8 cups whole milk

1 cup plain whole milk yogurt

1/2 cup heavy cream (optional for richer cheese)

2 tsp white wine vinegar or lemon juice

Method

Heat milk, yogurt and cream (if using) and vinegar in a heavy-bottomed saucepan.

Bring to boil on medium heat. Turn heat to low and

boil very gently for 2 minutes, or until milk is curdled. Remove from heat. Line a sieve or colander with 2 layers of clean cheesecloth or fine washed muslin. Set the colander into a deep bowl. Pour the milk mixture into the lined colander or sieve. Drain for 15 minutes. Pull sides of the cloth together and squeeze the curds gently to remove the whey (liquid). Remove strained curds from cloth and serve. You can store the ricotta cheese, in a covered container in the fridge for up to 3 days.

Crème Fraiche

Naturally soured fresh cream you can flavor with lemon zest, vanilla, or spices and use on top of fresh fruit for dessert.

Method

Stir 2 parts of fresh double cream with 1 part buttermilk, sour cream or yogurt (with live cultures). Stir over low heat until just warm. Allow to sit at room temperature for 6-8 hours. Stir and chill. Store covered in the fridge. Keeps for up to 3 weeks.

COOKING BASICS

Tomato Salsa

Per Serving: Sodium 8mg

Ingredients

6 medium tomatoes

2 spring onions

30 ml (2 tbsp) lemon juice

1 tbsp parsley, chopped

10 cm length cucumber, diced

2 tbsp coriander

Chopped pepper

Method

Skin and seed tomatoes. Dice. Mix all ingredients together and chill 1-2 hours.

Serve with toasted pita bread chips.

Per Serve: Fat 0.3g Cholesterol 0mg Sodium 8mg Potassium 317mg Carbohydrates 5.3g Fiber 1.7g Sugars 3.4g Protein 1.3g

Health Benefits Of Cucumber:
Rehydrates and helps eliminate toxins. B vitamins

Mango Salsa

Per Serving: Sodium Free

Ingredients

2 cups mango, cubed

1 onion, chopped

3 tbsp onion, chopped

3 tbsp oil

1 tbsp water

Mint leaves or coriander leaves

Lime juice

Method

Place mango in a mixing bowl. Combine onion, oil and water in a saucepan. Cover and simmer on low heat for 10 minutes. Add mango. Add 1 tbsp fresh mint or coriander leaves. Stir in lime juice.

Per serve | Fat 3.5g | Cholesterol 0mg | Sodium 0mg | Potassium 34mg | Carbohydrates 2.2g | Fiber 0.5g | Sugars 1.0g | Protein 0.2g |

Dukkah

Per Serving: Sodium 2mg

Ingredients

25g hazelnuts

25g almonds

1 tbsp smoked paprika

1 tbsp ground black pepper

3 tsp coriander seeds, roasted

2 tbsp thyme leaves

2 tsp garlic powder

Method

Roast nuts for 7-10 minutes. Put spices on a paper-lined baking sheet. Roast for 10 minutes, stirring frequently. Cool. Finely chop all in blender. Use as a healthy dip with yogurt; add to cooked vegetables; sprinkle over salad; coat potatoes before roasting; rub over meat or chicken before grilling or toss in cooked chickpeas for a salad.

Per Serve | Fat 4.9g | Cholesterol 0mg | Sodium 2mg | Potassium 118mg | Carbohydrates 4.2g | Fiber 2.1g | Sugars 0.7g | Protein 2.0g |

Health Benefits Of Hazelnuts:
Rich in vitamin B complex. Helps the nervous system function and helps with stress, anxiety and depression.

Orange Oil

Combine 500ml strained orange juice and 50ml strained lemon juice into a saucepan. Reduce over low medium heat until syrup-like. Cool to room temperature then whisk in an equal quantity of olive oil. Store in clean bottles. Use to drizzle over grilled fish, potatoes, salads and steamed vegetables, such as asparagus and broccoli.

Prawn Oil

Take shells from prawns you peeled. Heat light olive oil in a frying pan. Add prawn heads and tails. Fry on low heat until prawns turn pink. Cook a further 20 minutes. Cool. Strain through kitchen paper. Discard shells. Pour oil into a clean bottle. Store in the fridge. Use when grilling fish or add with lime juice and black pepper to make a dressing for seafood salad or Asian noodle salad.

SALT SUBSTITUTES

The new salt is a garden of herbs.

Think of fresh herbs as 'the new salt'. There is an old Chinese saying, if you want to be happy all your life, plant a garden. I would add to that, plant a herb garden. Just a couple of pots or a planter box of herbs will make everything you cook taste so much better. Just a teaspoon of herbs can make food taste fresh and enlivened, giving depth and richness to stews, soups, casseroles and sauces. Seriously, there is nothing as wonderful as the scent of fresh herbs. You can put the herbs in a shaker and use them at the table instead of salt. Use as a rub for meats and chicken. Add herbs to cooked vegetables. Add to sour cream for baked potatoes. Add to yogurt or soft cheeses for a tasty dip or dressing.

Rosemary, sage, oregano and marjoram are easy to grow. If they have enough sun, they will grow on a windowsill for months and you can use them everyday. When you trim them, they will keep growing until late season. You can use fresh herbs from your garden or bought from the store and then dry them in a low oven turned off, overnight. Fill your pantry jars and tins with herb seasonings and add zest to everything you cook. Herb blends enhance foods such as fish, chicken, beef and vegetables. Piquant blends such as dill, savory, thyme and garlic can help you eliminate salt without loss or flavor or taste. Here are easy to make blends.

French Blend

Per Serving: Sodium 2mg

Makes: 1/3 cup

Ingredients

2 tbsp dried dill

2 tbsp dried chives

1 tbsp dried oregano

2 tsp celery seeds

1/2 tsp ground black pepper

Method

Place ingredients into a blender. Process untill the herbs are well mixed together.

Per Serve | Total Fat 0.2g | Cholesterol 0mg | Sodium 2mg | Potassium 37mg | Carbohydrates 0.9g | Protein 0.3g |

Spice Island Blend

Per Serving: Sodium 2mg

Makes: 1/3 cup

Ingredients

1 tbsp ground cloves

1 tbsp cracked black pepper

1 tbsp crushed coriander seeds

1/2 tsp garlic powder

Method

Mix together and store in a cool place.

Per Serve | Fat 0.1g | Cholesterol 0mg | Sodium 2mg | Potassium 17mg | Carbohydrates 0.9g | Protein 0.1g |

Moroccan Blend

Per Serving: Sodium 2mg

Ingredients

3 tbsp ground cinnamon

1 1/2 tbsp ground black pepper

1 1/2 tbsp ground white pepper

2 1/2 tsp ground nutmeg

2 1/2 tsp ground cloves

2 1/2 tsp ground cardamom

Method

Mix together and store in a cool place.

**Per Serve | Fat 0.1g | Cholesterol 0mg | Sodium 2mg |
| Potassium 17mg | Carbohydrates 0.9g | Protein 0.1g |**

Chicken Herbs

Per Serving: Sodium 2mg

Ingredients

1 tbsp dried marjoram

2 tbsp dried tarragon

1 tbsp dried basil

1 tbsp dried rosemary

1 tsp paprika

Mix well and store in a jar.

Per Serve | Fat 0.1g | Cholesterol 0mg | Sodium 2mg | Potassium 17mg | Carbohydrates 0.9g | Protein 0.1g |

F i s h   H e r b s

Per Serving: Sodium 2mg

Ingredients

3 tbsp dill

2 tbsp dried basil

1 tbsp dried tarragon

1 tbsp lemon thyme

1 tbsp dried parsley

1 tbsp dried chervil

Mix well and store in a jar.

Per Serve | Fat 0.1g | Cholesterol 0mg | Sodium 2mg | Potassium 17mg | Carbohydrates 0.9g | Protein 0.1g |

Pork Herbs

Per Serving: Sodium 2mg

Ingredients

3 tbsp ground coriander

2 tbsp ground cumin

1 tbsp ground ginger

2 tbsp dried sage

1 tbsp dried thyme

Mix well and store in a jar.

Per Serve | Fat 0.1g | Cholesterol 0mg | Sodium 2mg | Potassium 17mg | Carbohydrates 0.9g
Protein 0.1g

Fine Herbs

Ingredients

2 tbsp dried chervil

2 tbsp dried chives

2 tbsp dried tarragon

2 tbsp dried parsley

Mix well and store in a jar.

Per Serve | Fat 0.1g | Cholesterol 0mg | Sodium 2mg | Potassium 17mg | Carbohydrates 0.9g | Protein 0.1g |

Bouquet Garni

Per Serving: Sodium 2mg

Ingredients

1/4 cup dried parsley leaves

4 bay leaves crumbled

2 tbsp dried thyme

2 tbsp dried marjoram

Method

Mix herbs together. Place 1 teaspoon in a small muslin bag or 6 cm square of cheesecloth doubled. Tie bag or gather up the corners and tie with kitchen string. Use in soups, stews and stocks.

Per Serve | Fat 0.1g | Cholesterol 0mg | Sodium 2mg | Potassium 17mg | Carbohydrates 0.9g | Protein 0.1g |

Italian Seasoning

Use on pizzas, pasta, herb bread, or any dish that needs Italian flavor.

Per Serving: Sodium 2mg

Ingredients

1/2 cup dried oregano

1/2 cup dried basil

1/4 cup dried parsley

1 tbsp fennel seeds, crushed

2 tbsp dried sage

1 tbsp red pepper flakes

Mix well and store in a jar.

Per Serve | Fat 0.1g | Cholesterol 0mg | Sodium 2mg | Potassium 17mg | Carbohydrates 0.9g | Protein 0.1g |

INGREDIENT KNOW HOW

Follow your instincts. Substitute one ingredient for another. Use other ingredients on hand, when you don't have exactly the right ingredients. The dish will be slightly different but still taste good. For example, if you don't have spinach, use rocket. If you don't have beans, use asparagus. If you don't have shallots, use red onion.

Basil goes with: Eggplants, Tomatoes, Olive oil, Lamb, Potatoes, Pine Nuts, Walnuts, Zucchini, Capsicum, Fish, Prawns, Pasta.

Bay leaves go with: Stocks, Soups, Dried beans, Lentils, Broad beans, Pork, Sweet peppers, Veal, Potatoes, Garlic, Onions, Milk

Coriander seeds go with: Beef, Lamb, Lentils, Mushrooms, Chickpeas, Eggplants, Chicken, Hazelnuts.

Chives go with: Chicken, Eggs, Fish, Potatoes, Cucumber, Celery, Beetroot, Butter, Eggs, Prawns, Fish,

Beef, Shallots, Garlic, Pork,

Coriander leaves go with: Prawns, Garlic, Pork, Beef, Avocado, Fish, Ginger, Coconut, Noodles, Soup, Mint, Parsley, Chicken, Yogurt

Fennel goes with: Olive oil, Lemon juice, Pepper, Chicken stock, Pasta, Olive oil, Tomatoes, Almonds, Walnuts, Fish, Garlic, Mushrooms, Chicken, Potatoes, Eggs, Rocket, Watercress,

Garlic goes with: Potatoes, Butter, Olive oil, Lamb, Pork, Veal, Fish, Shellfish, Basil, Rosemary, Fennel, Parsley, Spinach, Saffron, Eggs

Ginger goes with: Nutmeg, Raisins, Honey, Cinnamon, Cardamom, Almonds, Cloves, Brown sugar, Aniseed

Honey goes with: Cream, Fruit, Dried Fruit, Cardamom, Cinnamon, Nuts, Chicken, Pork, Ginger, Cloves, Dried beans

Lemons go with: Fish, Veal, Chicken, Shellfish, Fish, Cream, Eggs, Oranges, Honey, Tea, Pasta, Noodles, Rice, Raspberries, Papaya, Coriander, Cumin Seed

Mint goes with: Lamb, Potatoes, Peas, Carrots, Tea, Lime juice, Garlic, Noodles, Bean sprouts, Pork, Cucumbers, Parsley, Coriander, Cracked wheat,

Oregano goes with: Tomatoes, Eggs, Dried Beans, Rice, Grilled fish, Lamb, Sweet Corn, Sweet peppers, Chicken, Lemons, Eggplant

Parsley goes with: Butter, Garlic, Pepper, Fish, Cream,

Pepper, Lemon juice, Pine Nuts, Beans, Eggs, Lentils, Chickpeas, Chives, Chervil, Tarragon, Olive oil, Pasta, Zucchini, Artichokes, Mint, Cumin, Radishes

Rosemary goes with: Lamb, Pork, Chicken, Potatoes, Bread, Olive oil, Garlic, Parsley, Onions, Tomatoes, Yogurt, Fish, Pine nuts

Sage goes with: Butter, Pumpkin, Olive oil, Veal, Chicken, Potatoes, Sweet potato, Pasta, Duck, Lamb, Lemons, Dried beans, Peas, Onions, Leeks

Salad greens go with: Potato, Pumpkin, Eggplant, Sweet Pepper, Beetroot, Onion, Garlic, Green Beans, Dried Beans, Asparagus, Artichoke, Chickpeas, Carrot, Broccoli, Prawns, Squid, Poultry, Egg

Tarragon goes with: Chicken, Fish, Egg, Shallot, Beef, Tomatoes, Mayonnaise

Vinegar goes with: Salad Greens, Cucumber, Strawberries, Peppercorns, Herbs, Fish, Olive oil

Almonds go with: Honey, Peach, Apricot, Vanilla, Cream, Chicken

Cashews go with: Coconut milk Beans, Cauliflower, Fish, Chicken, Almond, Rice

Coconut goes with: Chicken, Fish, Beef, Rice, Turmeric, Kaffir Lime, Lemongrass

Hazelnuts go with: Almond, Pork, Duck, Cinnamon, Orange

Peanuts go with: Pork, Chicken, Beef, Cucumber, Beans

Pecans go with: Garlic, Maple Syrup, Lemon Juice, Molasses, Pine nuts, Basil, Veal, Pasta, Garlic, Rice, Salad, Lime

Pistachios go with: Rice, Yogurt, Honey, Semolina, Almond, Walnut, Pears, Garlic, Croutons, Cream

PASTA AND RICE

Pepper Pesto With Linguine

Per Serving: Sodium 26mg

Ingredients

400g dried linguine pasta

3 red capsicums

2 cloves garlic, peeled

25g basil leaves

70g roasted hazelnuts

4 tbsp extra virgin olive oil

Method

Heat oven to 200 C.

Make pesto: place capsicum on an oven tray. Roast 20-25 minutes, until charred. Place in a plastic bag to sweat. Slip off the skins. Deseed. Place basil, nuts and garlic in a food processor. Pulse to a course paste. Slowly add oil. Add capsicum and process until smooth. Add extra oil if needed. Cook linguine according to the instructions on the packet. Drain. Toss in the red pepper pesto. Season to taste with black pepper and shredded basil leaves.

Makes 4 servings | Serving Size 230 g
Amount Per Serving | Calories 618 | Total Fat 26.7g | Cholesterol 0mg | Sodium 4mg | Potassium 332mg | Carbohydrates 84.0g | Sugars 6.3g | Protein 16.3g |

Good points | No cholesterol | Very low in sodium | Very high in vitamin C |

Fresh Tomato Pasta Sauce

Per Serving: Sodium 26mg

Ingredients

6-8 ripe Roma (acid free) tomatoes

2 tbsp extra virgin olive oil

Freshly ground black pepper

1 clove garlic, crushed, garlic,

Bunch small fresh basil, washed, leaves only

Spaghetti, 100g per person

Method

Heat water to boiling. Turn off heat. Carefully drop the tomatoes into the boiled water for 30 seconds. Lift tomatoes out. Peel skin. Cut tomatoes in half. Squeeze out the seeds. Discard. Chop tomatoes into small pieces. Place olive oil, pepper, garlic and tomatoes into a bowl. Add torn basil leaves. Leave for 1 hour in the fridge. Cook pasta according to the directions on the packet. Drain pasta.

Place into serving bowls. Add tomato sauce and shredded basil leaves.

Makes 6 servings | Serving Size 237 g
Amount Per Serving | Calories 263 | Total Fat 6.5g | Cholesterol 49mg | Sodium 26mg | Potassium 514mg | Carbohydrates 43.2g | Sugars 4.3g | Protein 9.1g |

Good points | Low in saturated fat | Very low in sodium | High in iron | High in thiamin | High in vitamin A | High in vitamin C |

Basmati Pilaf

Per Serving: Sodium 10mg

Ingredients

1 tbsp extra virgin olive oil

3cm cinnamon stick

2 whole green cardamom pods

1/2 cup thinly sliced onions

1 cup basmati rice, rinsed and drained

1 1/2 cups water

Method

Heat oil in a medium saucepan over high heat. Add whole spices and cook, stirring until they make a popping sound. Add onion. Cook 2 minutes until translucent. Stir in rice and cook 1 minute, until fragrant.

Add water and bring to boil. Reduce heat to low. Cover pan tightly. Simmer about 15 minutes until water is absorbed. Remove pan from heat. Leave covered for 10-15 minutes.

Makes 4 servings | Serving Size 228 g

Amount Per Serving | Calories 445 | Total Fat 4.6g | Saturated Fat 0.8g | Cholesterol 0mg | Sodium 10mg | Potassium 270mg | Carbohydrates 97.5g | Sugars 1.3g | Protein 8.0g |

Good points | Low in saturated fat | No cholesterol | Very low in sodium | Very low in sugarHigh in dietary fiber | Very high in manganese | Very high in vitamin B6 |

Spicy Couscous

Per Serving: Sodium 61mg

Ingredients

2 cups instant couscous

25g unsalted butter

1 onion, diced

2 cloves garlic, crushed

1 tbsp ginger, finely chopped

1 tsp ground cumin seeds

1 tsp ground coriander seeds

1 tsp turmeric powder

1/2 tsp ground chili (optional)

1 cup nuts (almonds, pine nuts, walnuts)

1 cup dried currants (or raisins)

1 cup pumpkin seed kernels

Fresh flat-leaf parsley

Method

Melt butter in a large frying pan. Sauté onion, garlic and ginger for 2 minutes on medium heat. Add spices and nuts. Cook for 1 minute. Add currants and seeds. Bring 2 cups of water to the boil. Remove from heat. Stir in couscous. Allow to swell for 2 minutes. Add chopped parsley and the spice fruit mixture. Stir well and serve.

Makes 4 servings | Serving Size 226 g
Amount Per Serving | Calories 829 | Total Fat 33.9g
Cholesterol 13mg | Sodium 61mg | Potassium 1003mg |
Carbohydrates 112.1g | Sugars 24.2g | Protein 26.5g |

Good points | Very low in cholesterol | Very low in sodium | High in manganese | Very high in vitamin B6 |

Easy Couscous

Per Serving: Sodium 19mg

Ingredients

2 cups couscous

2 cups homemade chicken stock (or water)

1 tbsp olive oil

1/2 cup raisins

Zest of 1 lemon

2 tbsp mint, chopped

2 tbsp dill, chopped

1 tsp paprika

1/2 cup slivered almonds, roasted

Method

Place raisins in chicken stock. Bring to boil over
medium heat. Mix the almonds, spices and lemon
zest with the couscous. Put couscous into a deep
bowl and pour in the raisin stock mixture. Mix well.
Cover tightly and let cool, without uncovering.
When cool, mix in fresh herbs, fluffing with a fork to

remove any lumps. Reheat when required. Serve with grilled or roasted meat such as rack of lamb or roasted chicken.

Makes 4 servings | Serving Size 244 g
Amount Per Serving | Calories 485 | Total Fat 10.2g | Cholesterol 0mg | Sodium 19mg | Potassium 444mg | Carbohydrates 85.3g | Sugars 11.3g | Protein 14.6g |

Good points | Low in saturated fat | No cholesterol | Very low in sodium |

Health Benefits Of Couscous:
High in selenium (protects the cells DNA from the mutating effects of toxins). High levels of potassium.

P o t a t o   C u r r y

Per Serving: Sodium 12mg

Ingredients

4 tbsp oil

1 clove garlic

4 potatoes, peeled and diced

1/2 tsp sugar

1 tbsp coconut milk

1 cup water

400g can no salt tomatoes, liquid reserved

2 onions, sliced

1/2 tsp ground cumin seeds

1/2 tsp turmeric powder

1/2 tsp cinnamon

1/2 tsp cardamom

1/2 tsp black pepper

1/2 tsp ginger powder

Method

Fry onion in oil on medium heat until transparent. Add garlic and spices. Cook for 2 minutes. Add potatoes. Fry 2 minutes. Add tomatoes and bring to the boil. Simmer 20 minutes or until potato is cooked. Serve with rice.

Makes 7 servings | Serving Size 256g
Amount Per Serving | Calories 186
Total Fat 8.6g | Cholesterol 0mg | Sodium 12mg | Potassium 697mg | Carbohydrates 25.4g | Sugars 4.6g | Protein 2.9g |

Good points | No cholesterol | Very low in sodium | High in potassium | Very high in vitamin B6 | Very high in vitamin C |

Coconut Jasmine Rice

Per Serving: Sodium 7mg

Ingredients

2 cups jasmine rice

1 cup coconut milk mixed with 1/2 cup water

2 lime leaves, chopped

1 small red chili, chopped

Method

The rule is for every cup of rice; use 1 1/2 cups of liquid. (You can vary the amount of coconut milk to water ratio to suit your taste). Cook rice in coconut and water according to the instructions on the packet (cooking time varies according to the rice you are using). Once the coconut rice is cooked, add spring onions and coriander. Stir with a fork. Then place lid on the saucepan and set aside for 10 minutes before serving.

Makes 6 servings | Serving Size 128 g

Amount Per Serving | Calories 310 | Total Fat 9.6g | Cholesterol 0mg | Sodium 7mg | Potassium 114mg | Carbohydrates 51.2g | Sugars 1.5g | Protein 5.0g |

Good points | No cholesterol | Very low in sodium | Low in sugar |

FISH

Fish In Grape Sauce

This dish can be made with any white fish.

Per Serving: Sodium 49mg

Ingredients

6 fillets firm white fish

Plain flour for dipping

1 large egg

30g unsalted butter

Oil for cooking

1 tbsp shallots, peeled, finely chopped

1 cup seedless green grapes

1/2 cup white wine

1/2 cup thick style cream

White pepper to taste

Method

Place flour on a plate. Season with pepper. Dust
fish lightly with flour. Beat egg. Dip fish into the egg.
Heat oil in a frying pan. Quickly fry the fish until just

cooked. Do not overcook.

Keep warm in the oven.

Heat butter in a saucepan on medium heat. Add shallots. Fry until golden. Add grapes. Add wine and cream. Increase heat. Cook stirring until the sauce reduces and is a thick, creamy consistency. Place fish on serving plates and spoon grape sauce over. Serve with mashed potatoes or rice.

Makes 5 servings | Serving Size 205 g
Amount Per Serving | Calories 274 | Total Fat 7.0g | Saturated Fat 3.5g | Cholesterol 46mg | Sodium 49mg | Potassium 105mg | Carbohydrates 23.3g | Sugars 3.3g | Protein 23.1g |

Good points | Very low in sodium |

Health Benefits Of Grapes:
High in potassium which helps regulate the body's fluid balance. High levels of vitamin C.

F i s h c a k e s

Soft centered and crunchy on the outside. Fish cakes can be easily made ahead of time.

Per Serving: Sodium 47mg

Ingredients

500g potatoes, cooked and mashed

650g cooked white fish, flaked

5 spring onions, finely chopped

2 tbsp flat-leaf parsley (or 2 tbsp basil)

Finely grated lemon zest

1 egg yolk, beaten

1 tbsp lemon juice

For Coating:

1 egg yolk

140g plain flour

1 egg, beaten

120ml milk

100g dry breadcrumbs

3 tbsp olive oil

Method

Combine potato, fish, spring onions, herbs, lemon zest, juice and egg yolk. Season with pepper. Shape into 8 fishcakes. Whisk egg and milk in a bowl. Coat each fishcake lightly in flour. Then dip in egg. Then into breadcrumbs. Refrigerate for 30 minutes before frying. To cook, heat olive oil in a shallow frying pan over medium heat. Cook fishcakes 3-4 minutes each side until golden brown. Drain on paper towels. Serve with lemon wedges and salad.

Makes 4 servings | Serving Size 246 g
Amount Per Serving | Calories 369 | Total Fat 15.0g | Saturated Fat 3.2g | Cholesterol 148mg | Sodium 47mg | Potassium 655mg | Carbohydrates 49.8g | Sugars 3.6g | Protein 9.9g |

Good points | Very low in sodium | High in vitamin C |

Fresh Fish With Lime Mayonnaise

Per Serving: Sodium 36mg

Ingredients

2 tbsp plain flour

Freshly ground black pepper

6 fillets boned, skinned white fish

1 egg

Homemade toasted breadcrumbs

2 cloves garlic

2 tbsp lime juice

1 tsp lime zest

3/4 cup homemade crème fraiche

Method

Make breadcrumbs by placing slices of bread on a baking sheet. Bake in a 180 C oven until bread is dry and golden. Cool. Place in food processor and process to bread crumbs. Set aside. You can store any leftover crumbs in the freezer.

Prepare fish. Season flour with pepper. Coat the fish in seasoned flour. Mix egg and milk together. Dip floured fillets into egg mixture and then dip into breadcrumbs. Place in fridge until needed. Meanwhile make the lime mayonnaise.

To Make Lime Mayonnaise: puree garlic with lime juice, lime zest and crème fraiche. Add pepper to taste. Set aside. Heat oil and butter in a shallow frying. Fry fish for 2 minutes each side, or until cooked. Remove from heat. Place on a serving dish with lime mayonnaise, salad and oven baked potato wedges.

Makes 4 servings | Serving Size 89 g
Amount Per Serving | Calories 79
Total Fat 4.5g | Saturated Fat 2.4g | Cholesterol 52mg | Sodium 36mg | Potassium 86mg | Carbohydrates 8.2g | Sugars 1.9g | Protein 2.5g |

Good points | Low in sodium | High in selenium |

Zoe's Beer Batter For Fish

Per Serving: Sodium 4mg

Ingredients

4-6 pieces fresh fish

250g plain flour

1 tsp sodium-free baking powder

1/2 cup beer

1 cup cold water

Light olive oil for frying

Method

Place ingredients in a bowl and whisk to make a smooth batter.

Heat oil in a pan. Dip fish fillets in plain flour to coat lightly. Dip in batter. Fry fish until lightly golden on both sides. Drain on kitchen paper. Serve with lemon wedges.

Serving Size 245 g

Amount Per Serving | Calories 348 | Total Fat 3.9g | Cholesterol 47mg | Sodium 4mg | Potassium 691mg | Carbohydrates 39.5g | Protein 34.6g |

Good points

Very low in saturated fat | Very low in sodium | Very low in sugar | Very high in niacin | High in phosphorus | Very high in selenium | High in vitamin B6 | High in vitamin B12 |

Poached Salmon Nicoise

Per Serving: Sodium 63mg

Ingredients

400g salmon fillets, boned and cooked

Small handful fresh basil

Small handful rocket leaves

3 large new potatoes, boiled, diced

4 eggs, soft boiled and cut in quarters

300g green beans, lightly cooked

Freshly ground black pepper

24 cherry tomatoes, halved

Vinaigrette Dressing:

12 tbsp olive oil

6 tbsp white wine vinegar

Black pepper

Method

Divide potatoes, beans and cherry tomatoes into 4 bowls. Season. Place dressing ingredients into a screw top jar. Shake well. Add a serve of dressing into each bowl.

Makes 8 servings | Serving Size 285 g
Amount Per Serving | Calories 358 | Total Fat 26.5g | Saturated Fat 4.2g | Cholesterol 104mg | Sodium 63mg | Potassium 779mg | Carbohydrates 17.9g | Sugars 3.3g | Protein 15.0g |

Good points | Very low in sodium | Very high in phosphorus | High in selenium | High in vitamin C |

Tahitian Kokoda

Marinated raw fish in coconut cream.

Per Serving: Sodium 20mg

Ingredients

600g fresh firm white fish

1 cup white wine vinegar

1/2 cup fresh lime or lemon juice

1 tbsp coriander leaves and stalks, chopped

1 fresh green chili, finely chopped

250 ml coconut cream

1 1/2 cups cherry tomatoes, halved

2 spring onions, thinly sliced

Pepper

Lime wedges for garnish

Method

Skin and bone the fish and cut into 2 cm cubes.

Sprinkle fish with vinegar and marinade 1 hour.

Rinse carefully with cold water. Drain on kitchen

towels. Place fish in a bowl and pour lime juice over. Add coriander and chili. Mix together well. Set aside in the fridge for 15 minutes. Add coconut cream, tomatoes and spring onions. Mix and season with freshly ground black pepper. Place on a serving dish lined with crispy cos lettuce leaves. Garnish with lime wedges.

Makes 6 servings | Serving Size 126 g
Amount Per Serving | Calories 116 | Total Fat 10.2g | Saturated Fat 9.0g | Cholesterol 0mg | Sodium 20mg | Potassium 249mg | Carbohydrates 4.7g | Sugars 2.7g | Protein 1.5g |

Good points | Very low in cholesterol | Very low in sodium | High in manganese | High in vitamin C |

Health Benefits Of Cherry Tomatoes:
These are miniature versions of beefsteak tomatoes and equally nutritious. Vitamin B6, vitamin A. Contain lycopene to protect the body from cellular damage, osteoporosis and skin damage from UV light.

Moroccan Fish

Per Serving: Sodium 4mg

Ingredients

800g fresh fish fillets
1 clove garlic, crushed
1/3 cup coriander leaves, chopped
1 tsp paprika
Juice of 1 lemon
1/2 cup olive oil
Oil for cooking

Method

Dust fish fillets with freshly ground pepper. Place in
a deep baking dish. Mix garlic, coriander, paprika,
lemon juice and olive oil together. Pour over the
fish fillets. Marinate in the fridge for 2 hours. Heat
oil in a pan. Cook fish a few minutes on each side.
Serve hot with lemon wedges. Serve with couscous.

Makes 4 servings | Serving Size 245 g

Amount Per Serving | Calories 443 | Total Fat 26.7g | Cholesterol 78mg | Sodium 4mg | Potassium 923mg | Carbohydrates 0.9g | Protein 49.1g |

Good points | Very low in sodium | Very low in sugar | Very high in niacin | High in phosphorus | Very high in selenium | Very high in vitamin B6 | High in vitamin B12 |

Health Benefits Of Coriander:

Rich amounts of vitamins A, C and K. Thiamin, riboflavin, folic acid, calcium, iron, magnesium and potassium. Helps regulate insulin levels and can help relieve headaches.

More
Fishy Ideas

Fish Burgers: Mince fresh tuna or white fish with fresh coriander leaves and a little grated ginger. Shape into burgers and grill on a barbecue or bake in a 190 C oven. Serve on grilled sourdough bread.

Marinated Fish: Take thick fillets of fish and marinate them in a little lime juice, some grated ginger, a shallot, finely chopped and 1 or 2 kaffir lime leaves, Steam fish in a bamboo steamer, fry or bake.

Baked Fish Fillets: Wrap fish in buttered tin foil or baking paper parcels and sprinkle with lemon or lime juice and any of the following spices.

Seasoning Ideas For Fish: Grated lemon zest, freshly ground black pepper, whole sprigs of herbs like dill, coriander, mint, spring onions, green peppercorns, flat-leaf parsley, grated fresh ginger, ground cumin, paprika, saffron, or Beau's blackened spices (recipe follows).

Beau's Blackened Spices

This is what Beau says about this recipe. "Whack em in a hot buttered frying pan with a hey ho. Turn them over and enjoy."

Per Serving: Sodium 9mg

Ingredients

2 tbsp sweet paprika

2 tsp onion powder

2 tsp garlic powder

1 1/2 tsp white pepper

1 1/2 tsp black pepper

1 tsp thyme leaves, dried

1 tsp oregano leaves, dried

Method

Place in a hot buttered frying pan and turn them over, until aromatic. Cool and store in clean jars. Dip small pieces of fish or chicken (no more than 3 cm sized pieces) into the spices. Drizzle with a little olive oil. Grill, bake, barbecue or fry.

Serving Size 35 g

Amount Per Serving | Calories 74 | Total Fat 2.2gCholesterol 0mg | Sodium 9mg | Potassium 468mg | Carbohydrates 15.8g | Sugars 1.9g | Protein 3.4g |

Good points | No cholesterol | Very low in sodium | High in calcium | Very high in dietary fiber | Very high in iron | Very high in manganese | High in magnesium | High in niacin | High in potassium | High in riboflavin | High in thiamin | Very high in vitamin A | Very high in vitamin B6 | Very high in vitamin C |

Salmon Orange Avocado Salad

Per Serving: Sodium 44mg

Ingredients

500g boneless salmon fillets

2 avocados

2 oranges

1 tsp orange zest, finely grated

1 red onion

Salad greens

Fresh coriander

Vinaigrette:

1 tbsp grated orange rind

1 clove garlic, crushed

4 tbsp olive oil

3 tbsp red wine vinegar

Freshly ground black pepper

1 tsp cumin seeds, toasted

Method

Sear salmon fillets on both sides for a few minutes. Allow to rest. Peel avocados. Cut into slices lengthwise. Peel oranges. Cut into segments removing any white pith. Peel onion and cut in very thin rounds. Wash lettuce leaves and shake dry. Make the vinaigrette dressing by whisking the olive oil with orange zest, garlic, vinegar, pepper and cumin seeds together. Place salad in a bowl and toss with this dressing. Arrange in a bowl or individual plates. Place salmon, avocado, orange and onion on top. Pour over any remaining dressing. Add coriander leaves to garnish.

Makes 6 servings | Serving Size 279 g
Amount Per Serving | Calories 373 | Total Fat 27.8g | Cholesterol 37mg | Sodium 44mg | Potassium 847mg | Carbohydrates 16.3g | Sugars 7.3g | Protein 18.4g |

Good points | Very low in sodium | High in magnesium | Very high in phosphorus | High in selenium | Very high in vitamin B6 | Very high in vitamin C |

Spicy Ocean Cod

Per Serving: Sodium 124mg

Ingredients

Cod or fresh firm white fish (180g per person)

100 to150 ml extra virgin olive oil (mild, low acid)

1 1/2 lemons

1 tbsp lemon zest, finely grated

10 shallots, peeled and finely sliced

4 cloves garlic, crushed

1 tsp cumin seeds, toasted and ground

1/2 cup fresh coriander leaves, chopped

1/4 cup flat-leaf parsley, chopped

2 pinches freshly ground black pepper

Method

Combine all ingredients (except fish) in a food processor or blender to make a herb sauce.

Cut 6 squares of foil, large enough to hold the fish fillets. Place a piece of baking paper on top of the foil. Coat fish in herb sauce. Place on the baking paper. Spoon any remaining sauce over the fish. Wrap each portion into a parcel. Refrigerate for 4 hours. Take fish out 15 minutes before you bake it. Heat oven to 200 C.

Place parcels on a baking tray. Cook for 10-15 minutes (depending on the thickness of the fillets). Take care not to overcook. Remove from heat. Sit in a warm place for 3 minutes. Unwrap carefully. Spread tabbouleh salad on a plate. Place fish on top, including cooking juices. Serve with crusty bread or pita bread.

Makes 4 servings | Serving Size 230 g

Amount Per Serving | Calories 486 | Total Fat 37.0g | Saturated Fat 5.3g | Cholesterol 83mg | Sodium 124mg | Potassium 495mg | Carbohydrates 5.8g | Sugars 0.5g | Protein 35.3g |

Good points | Low in sodium | Very low in sugar | High in selenium |

MEAT AND POULTRY

Pork With Prunes

Per Serving: Sodium 89mg

Ingredients

1.5 kg pork, shoulder, cut in 4 cm pieces

1 bay leaf

1 sprig fresh sage

1/2 tsp ground black pepper

Olive oil for cooking

2 medium brown onions, peeled, cut in chunks

1 1/2 tbsp fresh ginger, grated

2 cups homemade chicken stock

100g dried prunes, pitted or dried apricots

1 small bunch flat-leaf parsley

2 tsp orange zest

1 orange, juiced

Method

Heat oven to 180C. Grind black pepper over pork.
Heat 1 tbsp of olive oil in a frying pan. Add pork

and cook on medium heat for 5 minutes, or until browned. Remove pork and place in an ovenproof casserole. Add onion and ginger to the frying pan. Cook 5 minutes. Add stock, sage, orange zest and juice. Bring to boil and stir brownings on the bottom of the pan, to enrich the flavors. Add prunes or apricots on top of pork. Pour frying pan sauce over pork. Cover with a lid. Bake in a slow oven for 2 1/2 hours. Serve with potatoes and green vegetables.

Makes 10 servings | Serving Size 243 g
Amount Per Serving | Calories 259 | Total Fat 5.6g | Saturated Fat 1.9g | Cholesterol 110mg | Sodium 89mg | Potassium 786mg | Carbohydrates 10.7g | Sugars 5.7g | Protein 39.9g |

Good points | Low in sodium | Very high in niacin | High in phosphorus | High in riboflavin | Very high in selenium | Very high in thiamin | Very high in vitamin B6 |

Prunes:
Rich in iron, potassium and fiber.

Pork And Veal Sausages

Per Serving: Sodium 77mg

Ingredients

1 tbsp olive oil

1 large onion, finely chopped

2 cloves garlic, finely chopped

2 tsp ground fennel seeds

1 tsp ground coriander seeds

500 g minced (ground) veal

500g minced (ground) pork

1/2 cup breadcrumbs

1 egg

Freshly ground black pepper

Method

Heat oil in a frying pan. Add onions and garlic and fry 5 minutes on medium heat until transparent. Take care not to brown. Add spices and cook for 2 minutes more. Cool.

Place onions and garlic in a large bowl. Add pork, veal, egg and breadcrumbsMix well. Season with pepper. Dust hands with plain flour. Dust a clean bench with flour. Break off pieces and shape into sausages. Leave in the fridge for 30 minutes to 1 hour. To cook, heat oil in a pan and fry, turning to cook until golden brown. Drain on kitchen paper. Serve hot with salsa or as part of a big breakfast with eggs, grilled tomatoes, grilled mushrooms, toast and homemade beans.

Makes 10 servings | Serving Size 122 g
Amount Per Serving | Calories 184 | Total Fat 7.4g | Cholesterol 105mg | Sodium 77mg | Potassium 416mg | Carbohydrates 1.8g | Sugars 0.7g | Protein 26.0g |

Good points | Low in sodium | Low in sugar | High in iron | Very high in niacin | High in phosphorus | Very high in selenium | High in thiamin | Very high in vitamin B6 | Very high in vitamin B12 | High in zinc |

Beef In Beer

Per Serving: Sodium 67mg

Ingredients

1 kg chuck steak, cubed

1 tbsp olive oil

350g onions, peeled, quartered

1 tbsp plain flour

450 ml light beer

1 sprig fresh thyme

1 bay leaf

1 clove garlic

Freshly ground black pepper

Method

Heat oven to 140 C. Heat oil in a pan. Add onions
and garlic. Cook 3 minutes. Remove onions and
garlic. Add meat to pan. Brown. Add onions and
garlic back to pan. Add flour. Turn heat down. Mix
flour with juices. Slowly add beer. Add thyme and
bayleaf. Cover pan. Place in oven. Cook 2 1/2

hours without removing the lid to keep flavors in. The meat should be tender. Serve with potatoes.

Makes 7 servings | Serving Size 261 g
Amount Per Serving | Calories 346 | Total Fat 9.2 g | Cholesterol 151mg | Sodium 67mg | Potassium 567mg | Carbohydrates 6.7g | Sugars 2.2g | Protein 52.3g |

Good points | Low in sodium | Low in sugar | High in selenium | Very high in vitamin B6 | High in vitamin B12 | Very high in zinc |

Slow Cooked Beef Stew

Per Serving: Sodium 76mg

Ingredients

1.5 kg chuck or blade steak

2 tbsp plain flour

2 tsp sweet, smoky paprika

425g can tomatoes

2 onions, peeled and diced

2 cloves garlic, crushed

1 stick celery, finely diced

3 carrots, peeled, cut in chunks

3 potatoes, peeled, cut in chunks

1 cup no salt beef stock or red wine

Freshly ground black pepper

Method

Heat oven to 180 C. Mix paprika and flour together. Coat beef in flour. Place in a casserole dish. Crush tomatoes with a fork. Add to meat. Add the rest of the ingredients to the casserole dish. Cover. Cook for 1.5 hours. Check meat is tender.

Makes 12 servings | Serving Size 273g
Amount Per Serving | Calories 313 | Total Fat 6.4g | Cholesterol 113mg | Sodium 76mg | Potassium 813mg | Carbohydrates 14.5g | Sugars 3.1g | Protein 46.9g |

Good points | Low in sodium | High in phosphorus | Very high in selenium | High in vitamin A | Very high in vitamin B6 | High in vitamin B12 | High in zinc |

Three Way Meat Stew

Per Serving: Sodium 93mg

Ingredients

1 kg chuck steak, cubed

1/3 cup organic plain flour

Pepper to season

2-3 tbsp olive oil

1 onion, diced

1 garlic clove, crushed

4 cups homemade beef stock

125g button mushrooms, washed

Method

Coat meat in flour seasoned with pepper. Heat oil in a frying pan and brown meat. Remove from pan. Add a little more oil and cook onion and garlic in the same frying pan until transparent. Return meat to pan. Add 1 cup of beef stock to the pan, stirring and scraping the bits off the bottom. Stir until the gravy thickens. Place in a heavy bottomed saucepan. Add 2 cups beef stock. Bring to boil. Reduce heat. Cook partially covered on simmer for about 1 hour.

Add mushrooms and reserved stock after 1 hour. When meat is falling apart and gravy is thick the stew is ready. Check seasonings. Serve stew as is, with potatoes or egg noodles.

Makes 8 servings | Serving Size 284 g
Amount Per Serving | Calories 388 | Total Fat 21.7g | Cholesterol 133mg | Sodium 93mg | Potassium 407mg | Carbohydrates 5.9g | Sugars 0.9g | Protein 40.0g |

Good points | Low in sodium | Very low in sugar | High in selenium | Very high in vitamin B6 | High in vitamin B12 | Very high in zinc |

To Make A Meat Pie

Use the stew recipe above to make the filling.

Method

Heat oven to 200 C. Cool the stew and place in a deep pie pan. Add a sheet of puff pastry on the top. Bake for 20 minutes until pastry is golden brown. Serve with no salt tomato sauce or relish.

To Make A Potato Top Pie

Method

Cool the stew and place in a deep pie pan. Cook and mash 5 potatoes. Place mashed potatoes on the top of the stew. Bake for 20 minutes, until the top is golden.

Health Benefits Of Mushrooms:

Helps your immune system and nervous system. Contains vitamin C, D, B6 and B12.

Perfectly Easy Roast Beef

Per Serving: Sodium 84mg

Ingredients

1.5 kg beef fillet

Black pepper

(Optional: Rub 1 tbsp of balsamic vinegar and
1 tbsp of pomegranate molasses over the meat
before roasting to create an extra savory glaze).

Method

Heat oven to 250C. Place beef in a roasting pan.
Rub pepper over the beef. Cook in a hot oven
for 20 minutes. Remove from heat. Allow to rest at
room temperature for 30 minutes or up to 2 hours.
Just before serving, heat through in the oven.
Serve with salad and roasted potatoes.

Makes 8 servings | Serving Size 188 g
Amount Per Serving | Calories 373 | Total Fat 9.4g | Cholesterol

168mg | Sodium 84mg | Potassium 62mg | Carbohydrates
1.9g | Sugars 1.4g | Protein 67.7g |

Good points | Low in sodium | Low in sugar | Very high
in iron | High in niacin | High in phosphorus | Very high in
selenium | Very high in vitamin B6 | Very high in vitamin
B12 | Very high in zinc |

Health Benefits Of Potatoes:
High source of potassium especially if you are using drugs for Meniere's that strip your body of potassium.

Shepherd Pie

Per Serving: Sodium 67mg

Ingredients

500g lamb or beef mince

1 large onion, finely chopped

2 stalks celery, finely chopped

2 carrots, finely chopped

1 tsp ground allspice

1 tbsp tomato paste

2 cups (500ml) beef stock

1 bay leaf

1 tbsp olive oil

Freshly ground black pepper

1 kg potatoes, peeled, boiled and mashed

Method

Heat oven to 180C. Heat oil in a frying pan. Add meat and cook until brown. Cook onion, celery, carrot and allspice 1 minute. Add tomato paste, stock, bay leaf and pepper. Simmer 20 minutes.

Place in baking dish. Top with mashed potato.
Bake until golden brown.

Makes 8 servings | Serving Size 250 g
Amount Per Serving | Calories 245 | Total Fat 5.1g | Cholesterol
56mg | Sodium 67mg | Carbohydrates 23.9g | Sugars
3.4g | Protein 25.1g |

Good points | Low in sodium | Very high in iron | High in
phosphorus | High in potassium | High in selenium | Very high
in vitamin A | Very high in vitamin B6 | Very high in vitamin
B12 | High in vitamin C | High in zinc |

Cajun Meatloaf

Per Serving: Sodium 86mg

Ingredients

1 tbsp extra virgin olive oil

2 onions, chopped

4 cloves garlic, finely chopped

1/3 cup no salt tomato paste

2 tbsp minced jalapeno pepper

2 tbsp oven dried tomatoes, finely chopped

1 tsp cumin

500g lean minced (ground) beef

750g lean minced (ground) turkey

1/2 cup breadcrumbs

1/2 cup milk

Method

Heat oven to 180C.

Heat oil in a frying pan. Add onions and garlic.

Cook 3 minutes. Place in a bowl. Add freshly

ground black pepper, tomatoes, tomato paste, cumin and jalapeno. Add minced beef and minced turkey, breadcrumbs and milk. Mix well. Grease a baking tin. Place meatloaf mixture in tin, smoothing the surface. Bake in oven for 1 1/2 hours until brown and crusty on the top. Remove from oven. Let sit for 10 minutes before serving with tomato salsa and salad with avocado dressing.

Makes 8 servings | Serving Size 219 g
Amount Per Serving | Calories 191 | Total Fat 5.6g | Cholesterol 58mg | Sodium 86mg | Potassium 305mg | Carbohydrates 9.2g | Sugars 2.6g | Protein 24.4g |

Good points | Low in sodium | Low in sugar | Very high in iron | High in niacin | High in phosphorus | Very high in selenium | Very high in vitamin B6 | Very high in vitamin B12 | High in zinc |

Sweet and Sour Lamb Casserole

Per Serving: Sodium 78mg

Ingredients

4 tbsp olive oil

2 onions, sliced

1.5 kg lamb shoulder, cubed

1 1/2 cups water

1/2 cup red wine vinegar

3 tbsp no salt tomato paste

2 tbsp sugar

3 tbsp pine nuts

3 tbsp raisins

1 tsp freshly ground black pepper

Method

Heat oil in a frying pan. Add onions. Stir. Cook until transparent. Remove onions with slotted spoon. Set aside. Add lamb to oil and brown lamb well. Place onions and lamb into a heavy bottomed casserole dish, preferably cast iron. Deglaze frying pan with a little water. Stir to absorb juices. Add deglaze liquid to casserole. Add vinegar, tomato paste, sugar and remaining water. Cover. Simmer on low heat for 1 hour. Stir occasionally. Add pine nuts and raisins. Cook 30 minutes until the meat is tender. Skim off any fat. Season with pepper. Serve with mashed potatoes, couscous, or steamed rice.

Makes 9 servings | Serving Size 263 g
Amount Per Serving | Calories 420 | Total Fat
16.6g | Cholesterol 150mg | Sodium 78mg | Potassium
701mg | Carbohydrates | Sugars 6.3g | Protein 47.7g |

Good points | Low in sodium | High in niacin | Very high in selenium | Very high in vitamin B6 | High in vitamin B12 | High in zinc

Health Benefits Lamb:
B12 for nerve function, B3 for the nervous system and high protein for energy.

Marinated Butterflied Lamb

Per Serving: Sodium 45mg

Ingredients

1.5 kg lamb leg, butterflied (bone removed)

Marinade

2 tsp ground cinnamon

1 tsp turmeric

2 tsp ground cumin

1/4 cup lemon juice

1 tsp ground nutmeg

2 tsp ground coriander

2 cloves garlic, chopped

1/2 cup olive oil

Lemon Dressing

2 tbsp mint leaves, chopped

2 tbsp coriander leaves, chopped

1 tbsp lemon zest

1/2 cup olive oil

Freshly ground black pepper

Salad

A handful of baby spinach leaves

Eggplant, roasted, sliced

Method

Combine marinade ingredients and mix well. Place lamb in an ovenproof dish. Pour marinade over lamb. Rub all over. Cover. Refrigerate overnight. Heat oven to 200 C. Place lamb skin side up in a roasting pan. Use the same marinade for basting. Spoon marinade over. Roast the lamb for 200 C for 35-40 minutes or until cooked. Remove. Let the meat rest for 10 minutes before slicing.

Make a salad of leafy greens and roasted eggplant. Place dressing ingredients in a screw top jar. Toss though salad. Serve lamb with lemon dressed salad and couscous.

Makes 4 servings | Serving Size 208 g

Amount Per Serving | Calories 483 | Total Fat 51.4g | Cholesterol 0mg | Sodium 45mg | Potassium 525mg | Carbohydrates 9.6g | Sugars 3.3g | Protein 2.8g |

Good points | No cholesterol | Very low in sodium | Low in sugar | High in vitamin A |

Jean's French Country Chicken Stew

Per Serving: Sodium 56mg

Ingredients

Free range chicken (5 drumsticks, 5 thighs)

Plain white flour

1 tbsp olive oil

1 tbsp butter

2 leeks, white part only, sliced

2 large carrot, chopped

4 stalks celery, chopped

1 1/2 cup no salt chicken broth

400g no salt Italian style tomatoes

4 medium potatoes, diced

4 sprigs fresh thyme

4 sprigs flat-leaf parsley

Freshly ground black pepper

Method

Wash chicken pieces and pat dry. Lightly dust with flour. In a large casserole, melt butter and oil together on medium heat on the cook-top. Add chicken pieces and brown. Remove from pan. Add leeks and cook on low heat for 10 minutes. Add carrots and celery. Cook 10 minutes. Add stock and let the stock come to the boil. Cook for 2 minutes. Add tomatoes, herbs and potatoes. Heat through. Add chicken pieces back to the casserole. Cover with a tight fitting lid. Simmer over low heat for 1 hour. Add thyme. Cook a further 1/2 hour, or until cooked.

Makes 8 Servings | Size 276 g
Amount Per Serving | Calories 164 | Total Fat 3.6g | Cholesterol 4mg | Sodium 56mg | Potassium 724mg | Carbohydrates 30.3g | Sugars 4.5g | Protein 3.8g |

Good points | Low in cholesterol | Low in sodium | High in dietary fiber | High in potassium | Very high in vitamin A | High in vitamin B6 | Very high in vitamin C |

40 Garlic
Roast Chicken

Per Serving: Sodium 94mg

Ingredients

1 large organic/free-range chicken

1 bay leaf

3 tbsp extra virgin olive oil

40 whole cloves garlic (3 heads) unpeeled

Thyme, rosemary, sage and/or parsley sprigs

2 red capsicums, deseeded, chopped roughly

2 celery stalks, roughly chopped

Freshly ground black pepper

1 1/2 cups homemade chicken stock

Method

Wash and dry chicken. Place 2 bay leaves inside the cavity. Heat olive oil in a large ovenproof casserole (one with a lid). Add garlic cloves, herbs, capsicums, celery and season with pepper. Cook on medium heat for 5 minutes taking care to brown. Add chicken stock and bring to the boil. Reduce heat to low and simmer for 5 minutes. Remove from heat and place chicken in the casserole, breast side up. Spoon herb and vegetable juice over the chicken to coat. Cover with a tight fitting lid and seal with kitchen foil to keep the juices in.

Bake in a 180C oven for 1 hour or until chicken is cooked. Remove chicken to a serving plate. Spoon vegetables around and spoon cooking juices over. Serve with crusty bread to dip in the juices.

Makes 6 servings | Serving Size 261 g
Amount Per Serving | Calories 283 | Total Fat 10.9g | Cholesterol 90mg | Sodium 94mg | Potassium 432mg | Carbohydrates 9.8g | Sugars 2.1g | Protein 35.6g |

Good points | Low in sodium | Low in sugar | High in niacin | High in selenium | High in vitamin B6 | Very high in vitamin C |

Lime Marinated Chicken

Per Serving: Sodium 85mg

Ingredients

1 kg chicken pieces

2 cups coriander roughly chopped

2 tsp whole black pepper corns

3 cloves garlic, peeled

5 tbsp lime juice

1 tsp grated lime zest

60 ml olive oil

Method

Slash the chicken pieces a little so the marinade will go into the flesh. Make the marinade. Process lime juice, coriander, peppercorns, garlic and oil in a food processor or blender until a smooth paste. Place chicken pieces in a flat oven dish. Spoon marinade over the chicken, coating well. Cover the dish with cling film. Leave in the fridge for 3 hours. Cook chicken in a 220 C oven for 30 minutes, turning to brown both sides during cooking. You can also barbecue on a hot grill.

Makes 6 servings | Serving Size 167g
Amount Per Serving | Calories 474 | Total Fat 17.1g | Cholesterol 193mg | Sodium 85mg | Potassium 558mg | Carbohydrates 4.7g | Sugars 0.8g | Protein 72.9g |

Good points | Low in sodium | Very low in sugar | Very high in niacin | High in selenium |

Chicken And Peach Salad

Per Serving: Sodium 85mg

Ingredients

1 roasted organic chicken

2 cos lettuces, torn into pieces

3 fresh peaches or 6 fresh apricots, cut in slices

2 spring onions (white part only), finely chopped

1/2 cup unsalted pistachio nuts, or walnuts

1/4 cup coriander leaves, roughly chopped

1/4 cup mint leaves, finely chopped

Orange dressing:

2 tsp cumin seeds, toasted

1 tsp fresh ginger, grated

2 lemons, juiced

1 tsp lemon zest

4 tbsp extra virgin olive oil

Ground black pepper

Method

Make orange dressing. Place ingredients in a screw top jar and shake. Set aside.
Prepare chicken. Remove meat from chicken and save bones and skin to make chicken stock. Discard fat. Shred chicken into bite-size pieces. Place in a serving bowl. Add dressing and toss. Add chicken. Place cos lettuce on a serving platter. Spoon chicken on top. Serve.

Makes 6 servings | Serving Size 167g
Amount Per Serving | Calories 433 | Total Fat 21.1g | Cholesterol 128mg | Sodium 85mg | Potassium 605mg | Carbohydrates 8.9g | Sugars 5.2g | Protein 52.0g

Good points | Low in sodium | High in niacin | High in selenium | High in vitamin B6

Health Benefits Peaches:
Contains vitamin C, A and fiber.

Baked Honey Lemon Chicken

Per Serving: Sodium 85mg

Ingredients

16 free-range chicken wings (tips removed)

125 ml lemon juice

6 cloves garlic, crushed

1/4 cup honey

Method

Heat oven to 200 C. Place wings in an oven baking dish. Roast for 30 minutes. Place garlic, lemon, honey in a bowl. Stir until honey is melted. Pour over wings and coat well. Return to oven and bake for 15 minutes until brown and cooked. Add a grind of black pepper. Serve with salad.

Makes 6 servings | Serving Size 167g
Amount Per Serving | Calories 430

Total Fat 7.8g | Saturated Fat 2.3g | Cholesterol 193mg | Sodium 85mg | Potassium 514mg | Carbohydrates 13.1g | Sugars 12.1g | Protein 72.9g |

Good points | Low in sodium | Very high in niacin |

Sophie's Chicken In A Pot

Per Serving: Sodium 100mg

Ingredients

1 free-range chicken

2 slices bread

1/2 cup milk

1 homemade no-salt spicy sausage

2 tbsp flat-leaf parsley

1 egg

1/2 tsp nutmeg, freshly grated

250g minced pork (chicken or veal)

6 carrots, peeled, cut in chunks

2 parsnips, peeled, cut in chunks

3 stalks celery, roughly chopped

2 leeks, while part only, sliced

2 small onions, cut in chunks

6 small potatoes, cut in chunks

Sprigs of fresh herbs (marjoram, rosemary)
Freshly ground black pepper

Method

Soak bread in milk. Squeeze dry.

Beat bread, egg, parsley, crumbled sausage, nutmeg, herbs sprigs and minced pork (or minced chicken, or veal) together. Wash and dry the chicken. Using the handle of a wooden spoon, carefully loosen the skin covering the breast to make a pocket for the stuffing. Stuff the bread mixture carefully between the skin and the breast. Place chicken in a large casserole with vegetables. Season with pepper. Add enough boiling water just to cover the chicken.

Bring to boil. Skim surface. Reduce heat. Simmer covered for 1 1/2 hours on low heat or until chicken is cooked. Remove from heat.

Carve in generous portions. Place vegetables on a serving dish. Place chicken pieces on top. Spoon stock over. Garnish with ground black pepper and fresh herb leaves. Serve this French country stew with crusty bread.

Makes 8 servings | Serving Size 363 g

Amount Per Serving | Calories 259 | Total Fat 2.5g | Cholesterol 53mg | Sodium 100mg | Potassium 1134mg | Carbohydrates 42.7g | Sugars 8.7g | Protein 16.9g |

Good points | Low in saturated fat | Low in sodium | High in dietary fiber | High in niacin | High in potassium | Very high in vitamin A | Very high in vitamin B6 | Very high in vitamin C |

Roast Chicken Salad

Per Serving: Sodium 158mg

Ingredients

1.5 kg free range chicken

4 cloves garlic, crushed

1 sprig fresh thyme

1/2 lemon

4 tbsp olive oil

Black pepper

Method

Heat oven to 200 C. Wash and dry chicken. Place
lemon, thyme and garlic inside the chicken.
Grind black pepper over chicken. Rub olive oil
over chicken. Place chicken in roasting pan breast
side down. Pour 1 cup of water over chicken. Roast
30 minutes. Turn chicken over. Roast a further 30
minutes. Baste often. Remove from oven. Take out
lemon and herbs and discard. Skim fat from pan.

Save meat juices. Set aside. Prepare dressing.

Roast Tomato Dressing

1/2 cup olive oil

Juice of 1/2 lemon

1/2 tsp sweet paprika

1 clove garlic, finely chopped

4 tomatoes

Method

Roast tomatoes at 200 C in a little olive oil until the collapse. Remove seeds. Place in a blender or food processor with paprika, garlic, olive oil and lemon juice. Puree until smooth. Add a pinch of sugar to taste and pepper.

Salad

Salad greens with your choice of ingredients. Roasted capsicums, or artichoke hearts; chopped cucumber, tomato and/or red onion. Fresh herbs: parsley, basil and/or mint leaves.

Place the salad ingredients together on a large platter. Cut chicken into large pieces and arrange on salad. Pour juices from roasting pan over chicken. Drizzle tomato dressing over.

Makes 6 servings | Serving Size 262 g
Amount Per Serving | Calories 461 | Total Fat 16.9g | Cholesterol
193mg | Sodium 158mg | Potassium 477mg | Carbohydrates
0.8g | Protein 72.6g |

Good points | Low in sodium | Very low in sugar | Very high in
niacin | Very high in selenium |

SWEET THINGS

Sydney Fruit Salad

Per Serving: Sodium 9mg

Ingredients

Rind of 1 lemon, cut in thin strips

2 cups water

400 ml orange or apple juice

2 tbsp sugar

1 vanilla bean, split in half lengthwise

1 tbsp fresh ginger, grated

2 stalks lemon grass

5 passion fruit

Selected fruit in season: Fig, Pineapple, mango, peach, strawberries, berries, kiwi fruit, banana, grapes

Extra mint leaves

Method

Put water, juice, sugar, ginger, vanilla, lemon rind, and lemongrass in a saucepan. Bring to the boil.

Simmer 15 minutes. Cool. Cover and refrigerate to chill, preferably overnight.

Place passionfruit in sieve. Discard pulp and seeds. Add passionfruit juice to the chilled syrup.

Cut fruit into pieces. Place in a serving bowl. Spoon lemongrass and passionfruit syrup over the fruit.

Makes 6 servings | Serving Size 254 g

Amount Per Serving | Calories 108 | Total Fat 0.4g | Cholesterol 0mg | Sodium 9mg | Potassium 312mg | Carbohydrates 26.9g | Sugars 19.7g | Protein 1.4g |

Good points | Very low in saturated fat | No cholesterol | Very low in sodium | High in dietary fiber | Very high in manganese | Very high in vitamin C |

Health Benefits Of Passionfruit:
Good source of dietary fiber, vitamin C, vitamin A and rich in potassium.

L e m o n
P u d d i n g

Delicious citrus self-saucing pudding.

Per Serving: Sodium 54mg

Ingredients

1 tbsp unsalted butter

1/2 cup sugar

2 tbsp plain flour

Juice of two lemons (or limes)

Grated rind of 1 lemon (or lime)

1 cup milk

2 large eggs (separated)

Method

Beat eggs and sugar until pale. Sift flour into the bowl. Add lemon juice and rind. Add milk and egg yolks. Whisk egg whites until they form stiff peaks. Fold gently into the egg yolk mixture. Pour into a buttered ovenproof dish. Bake in a pre-heated 180 C oven for 25-30 minutes until golden on top. The pudding has a warm citrus sauce underneath.

Makes 6 servings | Serving Size 90 g
Amount Per Serving | Calories 134 | Total Fat 4.3g | Cholesterol
63mg | Sodium 54mg | Potassium 65mg | Carbohydrates
22.0g | Sugars 19.0g | Protein 3.6g |

Good points | Low in sodium | High in vitamin B6 |

Perfect Upside Down Cake

Per Serving: Sodium 77mg

Ingredients

2/3 cup sugar

1/2 cup water

1 cup fresh fruit (plums, raspberries, strawberries)

130g unsalted butter

1/2 cup castor sugar

3/4 cup flour

1 tsp sodium-free baking powder

2 tbsp ground almonds

1 tbsp Cointreau liqueur or 1 tsp vanilla extract

Method

Place sugar and water in a pan and stir over low heat until sugar dissolves. Increase heat and boil syrup until it turns golden. Pour into a greased cake tin 20 cm, coating the bottom of the tin.

Place fruit on top of the caramel.

Cream butter and sugar together. Add eggs. Beat well. Sift flour and baking powder. Fold into the egg mixture. Add almonds, liqueur or vanilla.

Spoon over the fruit. Bake in a preheated oven at 190 C for 40-45 minutes until golden. Cool a little.

Tip the cake out onto a serving plate. Serve warm.

Makes 6 servings | Serving Size 102 g
Amount Per Serving | Calories 320 | Total Fat 18.8g | Cholesterol 47mg | Sodium 77mg | Potassium 69mg | Total Carbohydrates 37.1g | Sugars 23.3g | Protein 2.5g |

Good points | Low in sodium

Sophia's Orange and Almond Pudding Cake

Per Serving: Sodium 46mg

Ingredients

4 oranges, whole, unpeeled

6 eggs

3/4 cup sugar

1 1/4 cups ground almonds

1 tsp sodium-free baking powder

Method

Wash oranges and place in a saucepan. Cover with water. Bring to the boil on medium heat. Tip out water. Replace with fresh water. Bring to boil. Simmer for 45 minutes, until soft.

Drain oranges in a sieve. Remove pips. Place in a blender and blend until smooth. Set aside. Beat eggs and sugar until pale. Add oranges, almonds and baking powder. Mix well. Pour into a lightly greased 18 cm spring-form baking tin. Bake at 180 C for 45 minutes to 1 hour. Test with a skewer. Cool cake in the tin. Remove from tin and serve.

Makes 8 servings | Serving Size 159 g
Amount Per Serving | Calories 247 | Total Fat 10.8g | Cholesterol 123mg | Sodium 46mg | Potassium 320mg | Carbohydrates 33.0g | Sugars 28.2g | Protein 8.2g |

Good points | Low in sodium | Very high in vitamin C |

Warm Fruit Crumble

Per Serving: Sodium 112g

Ingredients

1/3 cup plain (all purpose) flour

1 cup organic rolled oats

2/3 cup soft brown sugar

1 tsp mixed spice

1 tsp cinnamon

1 tbsp ground hazelnuts

1/2 cup walnuts or almonds, chopped

100g unsalted butter, softened

Fruit: 6 (granny smith) sweet green apples, peeled and thinly sliced mixed with 1/3 cup sugar and the pulp of 6 passionfruit.

You can also use combinations of fruit. Replace apples in the recipe with any of the following fillings: 2 cups stewed or pureed fruit in season. Rhubarb, plums, apricots, peaches or fresh berries.

Method

Preheat oven to 180 C. Place fruit in a buttered dish with 1/2 cup of the juice. Place remaining ingredients in a bowl. Using your fingers, 'crumble' the mixture until it resembles soft breadcrumbs. Place on top of fruit. Bake 40 minutes until crumbs are golden. Serve hot with Eve's vanilla custard.

Eve's Vanilla Custard

800 ml milk

2 tbsp plain flour

1 tsp cornflour

1/3 cup sugar

1 egg

1 tbsp unsalted butter

1 tsp unsalted butter (extra)

1 vanilla bean pod, cut in half lengthways

Method

Heat milk and vanilla bean slowly in a double boiler pan on low heat. Mix flour, sugar, cornflour, egg and butter in a bowl to make a thick paste. Add 3 tablespoons of the warm milk and whisk in. Add 3 more tablespoons to the paste. Whisk again. Do this again until you have a thin paste. Remove vanilla pod from pan and scrape seeds with a knife. Discard pod and place seeds back into the milk. Add the thin paste to heated milk.

Stir until the custard starts to thicken. If becoming too thick, remove the pan from the heat. Keep stirring to avoid lumps. If you get a few lumps, whisk to remove them. Once thickness is achieved, add the teaspoon of butter and stir in. Serve immediately or cover in the fridge with plastic wrap. You can set this as a pudding; use in flans or in a ramekin as you would a crème caramel.

Makes 6 servings | Serving Size 258 g
Amount Per Serving | Calories 464 | Total Fat 21.4g | Cholesterol 36mg | Sodium 112mg | Potassium 338mg | Carbohydrates 68.1g | Sugars 46.0g | Protein 5.8g |

Good points | Low in sodium |

MEASUREMENTS

Oven Temperatures

Degree F		Degree C
200	=	100
225	=	110
250	=	120
275	=	140
300	=	150
325	=	160
350	=	180
375	=	190
400	=	200
425	=	220
450	=	230
475	=	240

Liquid Measures

1 tsp	=	5 mls
1 tbsb	=	20 mls
4 cups	=	1 liter
1/2 cup	=	125 mls

Solid measures

32 oz	=	1 kilogram
16 oz	=	500 grams
8oz	=	250 grams
7oz	=	220 grams
6 oz	=	185 grams
5 oz	=	155 grams
4 oz	=	125 grams
3 oz	=	90 grams
2 oz	=	60 grams
1 oz	=	30 grams

COOKING MEASUREMENTS

Liquids

1 tsp equals 5mls
1 tbsp equals 20mls
4 cups equals 1 liter
1/2 cup equals 125mls

Weights

32oz equals 1 kilogram
16oz equals 500grams
8 oz equals 250grams
7 oz equals 220 grams
6oz equals 185 grams
5 oz equals 155 grams
4 oz equals 125 grams
3 oz equals 90 grams
2 oz equals 60 grams
1 oz equals 30 grams

1 cup = Equivalent

1 cup oats = 100 g
1 cup corn flour = 190 g
1 cup whole nuts = 150g
1 cup chopped nuts = 125 g
1 cup unbleached plain flour = 155g
1 cup wholemeal flour = 155g
1 cup shredded coconut = 90 g
1 cup raw sugar = 250 g

Glossary

Al Dente: Cooked until tender but firm to the bite. A term used to describe perfectly cooked pasta.

Baking Soda: Bicarbonate of soda, raising agent. Substitute regular baking soda for sodium-free baking soda. Low sodium content baking soda is available in supermarkets, specialty food stores and health food stores.

Baking Powder: Most commercial baking powders contain sodium aluminum sulphate, although brands such as Haine Featherweight Baking Powder *contain 0 mg per 1/4 teaspoon.*

You can make a baking powder substitute at home by mixing 1/2 teaspoon cream of tartar with 1/4 teaspoon of low sodium baking soda. Use to replace 1 teaspoon of baking powder in recipes. There is a site selling sodium-free and low sodium products online at healthyheartmarket.com.

Beetroots: Beets.

Balsamic Vinegar: A superior vinegar using a centuries old Italian technique. Aromatic, spicy and sweet sour taste.

Borlotti Beans: Small, speckled beans that are pale

pinkish in color.

Bulgur Wheat: Dried cracked wheat.

Buttermilk: Makes baking lighter. You can make you own version simply by mixing 1 cup of milk and 1 tbsp of lemon juice.

Cake Tin: Cake/baking pan.

Chickpeas: Garbanzo beans.

Citrus Zest: The finely grated rind of citrus fruit. 1 lime = 1 tsp (teaspoon) of grated zest; 1 lemon = 2 tsp zest; I orange = 1 tbsp (tablespoon) zest; the juice of 1 lime = about 2 tbsp and the juice of 1 lemon = 4 tbsp or 1/4 cup.

Cos Lettuce: Romaine lettuce.

Coriander: Cilantro.

Cornflour: Cornstarch.

Creme Fraiche: Similar in flavor to sour cream. Used in both sweet and savory dishes.

Essence: Extract.

Eggplant: Aubergine.

Flour: Plain = standard flour.

Frying Pan: Skillet/frypan.

Ginger: 2 cm ginger root = 1 tsp finely grated ginger or 1 tbsp roughly grated.

Green Prawns: Raw prawns. Keep a bag in the freezer for quick meals.

Grill: Broil. To cook under the top oven element, or on the barbecue grill.

Hard-boiled Egg: Hard-cooked egg.

Icing Sugar: Confectioners sugar.

Kaffir Lime Leaves: Dark green glossy leaves add a citrus flavor. Shred and add to Asian style dishes.

King Prawns: Jumbo shrimp/scampi.

Lemongrass: A thick stalk with fragrant flavor. Easily found in most supermarkets. Be sure to peel away the tough outer layers of the stalk and use the tender parts.

Mascarpone: A fresh Italian cream cheese that can be used in both sweet and savory dishes. Follow the recipe in the book to save money and make your own salt free version at home.

Minced Meat: Ground meat

Mozzarella: Italian style cheese. See the recipe in this book and make your own at home.

Oven Temperatures: Oven temperatures vary depending if your oven is fan baked or not. Use cooking times as a guide. Check oven-baked dishes during cooking when trying a recipe for the first time. Always preheat your oven to start.

Passata: A brand name for tomatoes that have been skinned, deseeded and pulped. Usually sold in tall glass jars. It is the same type of puree you get if you mash canned tomatoes with a fork.

Pine Nuts: Seeds of the stone pine. Small, nutty and creamy tasting. Buy in small quantities and keep in the fridge to prevent them going rancid.

Polenta: Corn maize from Italy. Rich and golden in color. Milder than cornmeal with a smooth texture. Red kidney beans can be used instead. Soak all dried beans overnight before cooking.

Pomegranate Molasses: Specialty ingredient from delicatessens and supermarkets.

Ricotta Cheese: Soft curd, low fat cheese. Use in savory and sweet dishes. Make your own ricotta by using the recipe in this book.

Rocket: Arugula, rocquette, rucola, rugula.

Roma Or Plum Tomatoes: Egg-shaped tomatoes with plenty of juicy flesh and a few seeds. Ideal for making sauces. My preference is for Italian style Roma tomatoes as they are less acidic. Add a pinch of sugar where tomatoes are acid. Always chose robust, flavorsome, ripe and red. A truss of organic tomatoes, fully ripened gives more obvious flavor to food than pale force ripened ones.

Seed: Pip.

Shallots: Small sized onions with a sweeter taste

than regular onions. Delicious whole or roasted.
can be chopped and added to sauces and salsas.

Simmer: To cook just under bpoiling point- small
bubbles may erupt in one place.

Smokey Paprika: A spice made from ground
capsicums(bell peppers). Adds a smoky flavor and
to barbequed, grilled or roasted meat, chicken
and vegetables. The Spanish paprika is the smoked
variety called *Pimenton* and is available in sweet
(dulce), moderate or sweet and sour *(agridulce)*
and spicy *(picante)*.

Spring Onions: Green onions or scallions.

Steam: To cook food in a rising steam.

Stock: Enriched 'cooking water' produced from
simmering stock ingredients. Using homemade
no salt stock from fresh ingredients makes all the
difference to your cooking.

Sweet Peppers: Capsicum/bell peppers.

Thai Basil: A stronger, peppery flavor compared to
Italian basil. Used in Asian style dishes.

Tomato Products: Canned Italian tomatoes are a
superior product, rich, sweet and full of flavor. Buy
reduced sodium or no salt cans.

Turmeric: An aromatic spice from the same family
as the ginger root plant, so you can use it in the

same way. Adds color and warm peppery flavor.

Vanilla: Use natural vanilla extract where possible. Use vanilla bean pods when heating milk. Scrape out the seeds and use with flavored milk for custards and desserts. Keep a pod in a jar of sugar to make vanilla sugar for baking and desserts.

Vermicelli Noodles: Thin noodles made from rice. Hydrate in water before you use. Add to salads and stir fries.

SALTLESS BOOKS

95992001R00093

Made in the USA
Middletown, DE
28 October 2018